The Candida–Yeast Syndrome

The spreading epidemic of yeast-connected diseases: how to recognize and deal with them

Ray C. Wunderlich, Jr., M.D.

KEATS PUBLISHING

LOS ANGELES

NTC/Contemporary Publishing Group

ABOUT THE AUTHOR

Ray C. Wunderlich, Jr. received his M.D. from Columbia University. He is board-certified by the American Academy of Pediatrics and the American College for the Advancement of Medicine and practices preventive medicine and health promotion in St. Petersburg, Florida. He is the author of many books on nutrition and health, most recently the Keats Good Health Guide, *Natural Alternatives to Antibiotics*. His other books include *The Natural Treatment of Carpal Tunnel Syndrome; Sugar and Your Health; Kids, Brains and Learning;* and *Help for New Parents and Parents-to-Be.*

THE CANDIDA-YEAST SYNDROME

ISBN: 0-87983-697-0

Printed in the United States of America

11 12 13 14 RCP/RCP 0 9

Contents

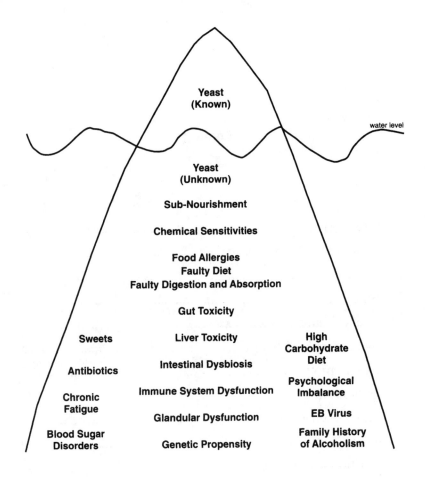

water level

Yeast
(Known)

Yeast
(Unknown)

Sub-Nourishment

Chemical Sensitivities

Food Allergies
Faulty Diet
Faulty Digestion and Absorption

Gut Toxicity

Sweets   Liver Toxicity   High
                                        Carbohydrate
Antibiotics   Intestinal Dysbiosis   Diet

                                        Psychological
Chronic   Immune System Dysfunction   Imbalance
Fatigue
                Glandular Dysfunction   EB Virus

Blood Sugar   Family History
Disorders   Genetic Propensity   of Alcoholism

Figure 1. **The "Iceberg" of Yeast Overgrowth.**
A host of associated conditions and disorders and practices is usually associated with the yeast connection; thus I term it the yeast complex. Sometimes the factors listed above precede or cause the yeast overgrowth; in other cases they result from yeast overgrowth. Thus food allergies may produce rhinitis and sinusitis that lead to the recurrent use of antibiotics, thus inducing yeast overgrowth that may, in turn, lead to additional food allergies. For each patient there is an individual set of particular factors.

INTRODUCTION

Orian Truss, M.D., of Birmingham, Alabama, was the first to make the breakthrough observations about the candida-yeast syndrome in the late 1970s and 1980s. William Crook, M.D., of Jackson, Tennessee, later studied, publicized and advanced the concept. Over the past 20 years, other erudite physicians have authored books describing it. The yeast connection now occupies center stage in the practices of nutritionally oriented doctors, nutritionists and many other therapists who see clearly the broad range of factors that account for so much of the misery that their clients experience. For better or worse, health food store personnel have become resident experts on the condition because of the flock of individuals who patronize their stores seeking relief when their doctors fail to provide help or brand them as hysterical, neurotic or misguided.

Thus, largely as the result of Dr. Crook's elaborate writings and lectures, we have a vastly informed public at the same time the bulk of the standard medical profession fails to recognize the yeast syndrome as a bona fide condition. In this booklet my intention is to describe the enormous impact of yeast overgrowth on health, the up-to-date methods of diagnosis and the broad treatment options available.

Figure 1 is a fairly comprehensive depiction of the "iceberg" that the yeast syndrome represents. It is a complex of conditions, a disease process that may be a primary or secondary disorder. The yeast overgrowth complex, silent or evident, usually manifests in the gastrointestinal tract. It is one of those conditions (of which there are many more) that often quietly produces over the years a load of unwanted chemicals, toxins, macromolecules or partially digested foods that, in turn, adversely impact the liver and other target organs. The brain, the thyroid and the adrenal glands are commonly involved. When the detoxication powers of the liver do not work properly, a host of xenobiotics (foreign chemicals) from the environment cannot be disposed of correctly by the body with the result that dysfunction and degeneration of body tissues occur. All this usually occurs gradually over months, years, even decades of life. One could make the case that the yeast-overgrowth complex may be the largest single factor in the production of the degenerative diseases that plague our aging society. The 1980s and 1990s have been the decades of proliferating autoimmune disease. In thyroiditis, lupus, rheumatoid arthritis, dermatomyositis, Alzheimer's disease and juvenile diabetes mellitus, for example, body organs or tissues are attacked by the body's own immune cells because they are not recognized as self. Something is very wrong with this scenario. I believe that the yeast complex, in conjunction with the load of xenobiotics in today's environment, plays an enormous role in setting up these conditions.

More must also be said about the immune system. When the limited supply of immune cells are busy reacting to yeast overgrowth, food allergens, harmful bacteria, and their toxic by-products, they are unavailable to wrestle with viruses, mutant cells and chemical pollutants. Thus immune decline may be present as a *cause* of the yeast complex (witness the near universal occurrence of candidiasis in AIDS as well as the inordinate frequency of high-titered EB-virus antibodies in the yeast complex) but also as a *result* of it.

I must admit that the scenario that I have presented is partially a result of my own conjecture. Nevertheless, every year, the worldwide medical literature continues to develop support for the disease-causing nature of intestinal dysbiosis and its harmful impact in the impairment of liver detoxification. A major component of the yeast complex is intestinal dysbiosis. And, a major component of intestinal dysbiosis is the yeast complex.

As one studies the yeast connection, one is struck by the rampant side effects of the chemical, dietary and antibiotic assaults made upon us since the industrial revolution, the introduction of processed foods and the medical profession's love affair with antibiotics. Lest I come across as a radical nihilist in human affairs, let me assert that the march of progress of civilization has at the same time provided us with amazing benefits. Yet I recognize too the enormous price that each of us has paid and is paying for the advances of civilization. Part of that enormous price is the yeast complex.

Candida Questionnaire

1. Have you taken antibiotic drugs frequently or over long periods of time?

2. Have you had recurrent skin, nasal, sinus, throat, ear, bronchial, lung, vaginal, prostate or urinary infections? Have you had severe infections such as osteomyelitics, bloodstream infection, or meningitis? Have you taken antibiotics with each dental cleaning or other dental treatments? Have you received antibiotics for treatment of acne?

3. Do you feel "sick all over" without obvious cause?

4. Are you troubled by hormonal disturbances accompanied by PMS, menstrual irregularities, low body temperatures or sexual dysfunction?

5. Do you eat a lot of sugar, alcoholic beverages, refined and processed carbohydrates, fruit juices, fruits, candy, carrot juice or other sweets? Do you crave sugar? Starches?

6. Are you bothered by chemical sensitivities (tobacco smoke, perfumes, cleansers, auto fumes, formaldehyde, etc.)?

7. Do you have short-term memory loss or "fuzzy" thinking?

8. Have you taken birth-control pills or corticosteroids over a long period of time?

9. Do some foods disagree with you or trigger your symptoms?

10. Do you have gastrointestinal symptoms such as bloating, gas, constipation, or diarrhea? Does your lower abdomen bulge more than it should?

11. Have you had athlete's foot, ear fungus, ringworm, "jock itch," or other chronic fungus infections of the skin or nails?

12. Are you diabetic? Have you had or do you have low blood sugar?

13. Do you have itching in your ears? skin? scalp? vagina? anus?

14. Do you have urinary symptoms (frequency, urgency, burning, etc.) without explanation?

15. Have you found that anti-yeast treatment measures have been helpful in alleviating unwanted symptoms or conditions?

These 15 questions are based upon the list originated by William Crook, M.D. and published in The Yeast Connection Handbook, *Jackson, Tenn.: Professional Books, Inc., 1997.*

THE CANDIDA QUESTIONNAIRE

Now let us look at my version of the landmark set of questions first composed by Dr. William Crook, and use them as a format for discussion of the factors that permeate and surround the yeast connection.

1. The repeated or prolonged use of antibacterial drugs. The use and overuse of antibiotics since their introduction in the 1940s has targeted those persons who, for one reason or another, are prone to yeast overgrowth. The yeast-promoting effects of the antibacterial drugs apparently occur not only because of direct yeast stimulation but also because of an ecological dislocation in the gastrointestinal tract when these drugs kill off the "friendly" bacteria. There are two sources of antibiotics: indirectly, from eating the flesh of animals whose feed is laced with antibiotics to promote growth; and directly, from the drugs prescribed by physicians to treat infections. Prominent among the infections for which antibiotics are used are recurrent conditions such as sore throats, sinusitis, middle ear infections, bronchitis, cystitis, urethritis, prostatitis and acne. Commonly, the underlying origins of these infections, such as allergies, nutrient-poor diets, environmental toxins and excessive amounts of sugar and chemically processed junk foods are not addressed. Very often, one requires the services of a physician who specializes in nutritional or preventive medicine in order to obtain a comprehensive understanding of the underlying causes of these infections and the many natural alternative methods that are available for managing or preventing them.

Dr. Crook indicated that 20 percent of yeast overgrowth is due to the improper use of antibiotics. I suspect that figure is too conservative.

2. Recurrent vaginal, prostate, urinary or other infec-

tions. The presence of such infections usually leads to extensive treatment with antibiotic therapy. Also, each of these anatomical sites in the body—particularly the vagina, the prostate and the urinary tract—may be the locus for yeast infection that rarely, if ever, is properly diagnosed. Because of the frequent use of the broad-spectrum drugs such as tetracycline in the treatment of acne, I would include that disorder as well.

3. **Feeling "sick all over" without obvious cause.** Despite the fact that literally hundreds of other causes may make one feel sick all over, most other conditions present accompanying symptoms or signs that point to the true origin of the malaise. Unexplained fatigue, tiredness, exhaustion or weakness are important indications of a possible yeast problem.

4. **"Hormone disturbances" such as PMS (premenstrual syndrome), menstrual irregularities and sexual dysfunction.** Why should chronic yeast overgrowth produce those disturbances? A properly functioning monthly cycle depends upon the smooth interaction of the neurological and endocrine-glandular systems as well as proper nourishment, absence of toxicity and psychological well-being. Emotional upset may be enough to alter a woman's cycle, and the presence of an infection such as yeast overgrowth in the body will certainly disrupt the monthly cycle.

Low body temperature also occurs in patients with chronic yeast overgrowth. However, it is also a prominent feature of some cases of malnutrition, hypothyroidism, low adrenal gland function and other conditions.

5. **Sugar cravings.** Sugar craving, of whatever origin, usually results in yeast overgrowth because of the chronic repetitive ingestion of sweets. On the other hand, the establishment and proliferation of yeast overgrowth in the body nearly always induces the craving for sweets. Therefore, a self-destructive cycle ensues in which the individual induces the disorder by eating too many sweets, and the resulting yeast overgrowth perpetuates the disorder by calling for the carbohydrate sustenance that it needs in order to flourish.

So-called "sweet-aholics" nearly always possess a yeast

infestation. Such individuals also often possess a host of other conditions such as intestinal parasitosis, malnutrition and body endotoxicity. The question of which comes first, the latter conditions or the yeast overgrowth, seems academic. As I have stressed in Figure 1, the process of yeast overgrowth involves a large number of associated conditions and disorders. If undigested and unabsorbed food, parasitosis, malnutrition and body toxicity are not initially present, they almost certainly will be in due time if the yeast complex is not properly identified and treated. In fact, I have come to know that the predominant cause of sweet and carbohydrate craving in our culture is unrecognized and unmanaged yeast overgrowth associated with malnutrition. Nevertheless, I am impressed with the will power of properly managed individuals to turn away from sweets and sugar after many decades of yeast overgrowth, even in the face of continued social temptations.

6. Chemical sensitivities. The flood of chemicals that abounds in today's environment exposes each of us to a cumulative load of pesticides, food additives and industrial chemicals never before experienced by man. As a result, certain individuals who are particularly susceptible develop either toxic conditions or hypersensitivity syndromes. Chronic yeast overgrowth is one of the most common responses in individuals who are acutely sensitive to chemicals in the environment. The symptoms of chemical sensitivity themselves are protean and include headaches, burning eyes, nasal irritation, sinus congestion and cough, as well as the systemic malaise of exhaustion, fatigue, weakness, irritability, mental spaciness and brain fog. The chemically hypersensitive individual may also be intolerant to noise, bright lights and crowds, and he may possess an erratic heartbeat. Many are acutely sensitive to the perfumes, paints, lacquers, smokes, colors, dyes, formaldehyde, lawn chemicals, rug-backing chemicals, out-gassing plastics and other petrochemicals that they encounter in everyday life.

The mechanism of the increased chemical susceptibility of the yeast-overgrowth individual is not known. Perhaps it is the cumulative load of the toxic exposures from within (yeast and its toxins) and those from without (the environment) that overwhelms the capacity of the individual to function in a normal manner. Or more specifically, perhaps the long-term presence of yeast overgrowth interferes with the body defenses that identify, detoxify and excrete foreign chemicals from the body. We do know that certain individuals are less able to manage the burden of foreign materials that surround them. Yeast overgrowth undermines their capacity to detoxify these substances.

7. Short-term memory loss and "fuzzy" thinking. When young people in their 20s, 30s or even 40s have difficulty recalling and there is no obvious cause, think yeast connection. Moreover, the successful treatment of the condition usually restores the memory to the grateful patient. Again, the mechanism underlying the memory disturbance occasioned by the fungal-yeast overgrowth is unknown, but the load of yeast overgrowth disturbances in the following loci are undoubtedly responsible: the gastrointestinal tract, the genitourinary tract, the respiratory tract and the skin.

8. Corticosteroids and birth control pills. The longer the birth-control pill is taken, the more likely yeast overgrowth will occur. Some persons require low doses of hydrocortisone or prednisone in order to function normally. Those persons do not usually have yeast overgrowth due to the corticosteroid drug. Persons treated with high doses, however, may well develop yeast overgrowth although the yeast promotion of corticosteroids appears to be less powerful than that of sugar, antibiotics, refined carbohydrates and birth control pills. The fact that all of the latter interfere with optimal nourishment is also contributory.

9. "Do some foods disagree with you or trigger your symptoms?" Food allergies and intolerances are rampant in patients with yeast overgrowth. The question also succinctly points to the observation that certain foods notoriously bring on or exacerbate the symptoms of yeast overgrowth. Besides sugars, these foods include refined carbohydrates, fruits and alcoholic beverages. Moreover, the yeast patient nearly always has food allergies. Often these are extensive. Commonly, yeast itself is one of the allergies. Hence the patient may react adversely to bread, alcohol and other fermented foods that contain yeast. While it is most important to avoid or limit the allergenic foods, one must be quite careful to maintain nutritional adequacy. Little is accomplished for the patient if the problem of food allergy is traded for malnutrition. The availability of excellent blood tests to uncover food allergies makes it easy to pinpoint and eliminate immune-based food reactions, thus allowing the healing energies of the immune system to address the yeast, bacterial and viral pathogens, foreign chemicals and any mutant cells that compromise the patient's health.

10. Gastrointestinal tract symptoms. These are a major component of the yeast problem. The presence of abdominal distention, particularly below the belt line, is a very frequent indicator of the presence of yeast overgrowth, especially in females. The degree of abdominal distention parallels the likelihood that significant yeast overgrowth will be found when careful stool culturing is carried out by a laboratory specializing in yeast diagnosis (see Resources), when blood tests for yeast are carried out or when therapeutic trials of anti-yeast treatment are given.

11. Athlete's foot and other chronic fungal conditions. The various skin disorders that commonly occur with the Candida-yeast syndrome also occur in a wide variety of other conditions. It is true, indeed, that such skin conditions alone are rarely indicative of a yeast condition. For example, allergies, nutrient deficiencies or autoimmune disorders may all cause itching, tingling, burning, dryness or rash. Not everything has its origin in yeast, but the exact limits of its reaches have not yet been drawn.

12. Are you a diabetic? I have found that patients with diabetes mellitus almost always have yeast overgrowth as well. Similarly, those who consume a high carbohydrate diet (fruit and fruit juices, refined breads, pastries, pasta and sweets) usually are found to have yeast overgrowth. The cholesterol scare so prominent in our country in recent years has undoubtedly been responsible for a rather marked shift away from the high fat and high protein diets of the past. The resultant turn to eating more carbohydrates has served, like the overuse of antibiotics, to promote the growth and overgrowth of yeast in the bowels of many Americans. The patient with yeast overgrowth will not recover until all craving for sweets and excess carbohydrates has been extinguished.

Those who habitually consume alcoholic beverages usually have low blood sugar. Conversely, persons with low blood sugar may seek out alcoholic beverages as one form of carbohydrate for sustenance. Most low blood sugar patients have induced their condition by overindulgence in sweets. Moreover, low blood sugar is a strong risk factor for eventual diabetes mellitus. The sugar connection with yeast is profound.

13. Itching. Itching in the skin, scalp, ears, anus or genitals is a very significant indicator of the presence of yeast overgrowth in the body. There are many other causes of itching, but yeast overgrowth in those areas is number one in likelihood today.

14. Urinary symptoms. Girls or women who on competent medical examination and testing are found to have urinary symptoms with "no cause" very often have yeast overgrowth. Sometimes the only way to prove that the urinary frequency, urgency, burning, blood in the urine or pressure are yeast-related is a therapeutic trial of treatment against yeast. Often, however, when cultures of the urine are repetitively examined—on special media that fosters the growth of yeast—the yeast presence in otherwise sterile urine can in fact be demonstrated.

15. Success with anti-yeast treatments. Because of the wide dissemination of information about the yeast condition in the lay community (largely as a result of the persistent and continuing efforts of Dr. Crook), many persons are familiar with effective self-treatments of their yeast condition. Health food stores, nutritionists, chiropractors, counselors, acupuncturists, massage therapists and others are often involved in spreading the word about the yeast "epidemic" in our society. Although there are some adverse outcomes because of some non-medically supervised therapies, most are successful. Sometimes physicians are also involved in these positive outcomes. For example, a gynecologist may prescribe the pharmaceutical drug fluconazole (Diflucan) to treat vaginal candidiasis with good results. He is usually reluctant, however, to open his mind to the fact that the condition amounts to anything more than a local occurrence of symptoms.

DIAGNOSIS

Someone once said that he didn't need a labeled road map in order to recognize an oasis in a desert when he saw one. Although mirages may occur, the oases that are seen by so many physicians today who accurately diagnose and treat yeast overgrowth lead to almost miraculous transformations in patients whose lives may have been miserable. Yeast treatments work—when the diagnosis is correct.

How then does one diagnose yeast overgrowth, the yeast syndrome? First of all, carefully. No patient wishes to embark on a futile series of tests and treatments and most physicians are sticklers for correct diagnosis. The lack of a certain blood test, x-ray, biopsy or a pathognomonic set of symptoms worries the conscientious physician who does not desire to become swept up in a popular, clinical disorder of disputed identity. Furthermore, nearly all physicians are taught that candida-yeast accounts for a few benign conditions such as infant thrush, diaper rash and temporary, post-antibiotic vaginitis. As for serious disease, their mentors, textbooks and journals recognize candida-yeast as a limited, opportunistic pathogen that overgrows in seriously ill, debilitated patients who have end-stage cancers or defective immune systems from radiation, chemotherapy, AIDS or corticosteroid drug treatments, often associated with indwelling catheters and malnutrition. It is ironical that such a standard medical position is both right and wrong. It is right in that faulty host resistance permits Candida-yeast to bloom and spread. It is wrong in that the miseries of the yeast connection are confined only to a largely hospital-based population of the seriously ill. The fact that the yeast syndrome has received such popular attention and has caught the fancy of the lay public seems to lead standard physicians to question its actual existence. After all, anecdotal data are regarded by the "scientific" community as notoriously unreliable. The result of such medical position-taking has split physicians into two camps: the larger conventional and standard group that views the yeast syndrome as largely a figment of the patient's imagination and the smaller more liberal group that recognizes a true oasis in a desert for what it is: a remarkable opportunity to assist those with yeast overgrowth to fuller and more enjoyable lives.

It is true that the diagnosis of the yeast syndrome is a *clinical* diagnosis. That means that the possibility of the condition has to exist somewhere in the mind of the supervising physician. Once considered a diagnostic possibility, the physician may proceed to assemble evidence to support or deny the possibility that the Candida-yeast overgrowth may account for the patient's signs and symptoms. What then are the factors that lead one to suspect the condition? There are four:

1. A compatible history
2. Positive findings on examination
3. Supportive laboratory data
4. A favorable response to treatment

The compatible history is a history that scores highly on the Crook questionnaire. That is, the patient has taken repeated or prolonged courses of antibacterial drugs or birth control pills or corticosteroids, he has diabetes mellitus, he eats a refined carbohydrate diet and so on. Also, the patient commonly has flatulence, anal itching, ear itching, poor memory or chemical sensitivities.

The positive findings on examination that almost certainly implicate yeast overgrowth are oral thrush; a thick, white, cheesy vaginal discharge; or characteristic fungal rashes. The Wunderlich sign of lower abdominal bloating must not be forgotten although it is not diagnostic of only this condition.

Laboratory tests can be most helpful in supporting the diagnosis of yeast overgrowth. A culture of urine may grow out yeast. So may vaginal, stool, mouth, gum, sputum and skin cultures. Whenever the Candida organism can be demonstrated to be present in abnormal numbers, the diagnosis of the yeast syndrome is strengthened. The absence of yeast growth in cultures, however, does *not* eliminate the possibility of yeast overgrowth. Special laboratory growth media will enhance the chances that Candida-yeast can be successfully harvested from the specimen submitted. It is true, however, that when a large number of attempts at culturing prove to be negative, the likelihood of yeast overgrowth as a cause of the patient's symptoms is reduced. If, however, one is obtaining cultures of the mouth and vagina but neglecting the stool, then no judgment can be made as to the absence or presence of yeast in the gastrointestinal tract.

The blood of the patient may also provide significant evidence for yeast overgrowth that has challenged the host's immune system. Candida immune complexes contain immunoglobulin G Candida antibodies, Candida antigen, and fragments of complement. According to Alan Broughton, M.D., of Antibody Assay Laboratories, (see Resources) immune complexes are present in proportion to the Candida load, and elevated levels are evidence of an abnormally increased yeast load in the body. Dr. Broughton finds that abnormally high Candida immune complexes have a 95 percent correlation with clinical symptoms of the patient. That is, only 5 percent of patients with positive immune complexes fail to manifest the typical clinical picture of yeast overgrowth. Furthermore, levels of immune complexes fall in direct proportion to the clinical improvement of the patient. My long experience with the treatment of yeast patients agrees with that pronouncement.

Elevation of IgA antibodies may occur in superficial yeast infections of the mucous membranes of the vagina, gut, urethra or in the skin. IgM antibodies rise initially and transiently in acute infections. Increased IgG antibodies are present in most adults and indicate past infection. I find that the IgG antibodies, when elevated, do become lower as the patient's symptoms improve under prolonged treatment. The candida antibodies, when compared to the candida immune complexes, lack the specificity for conclusive diagnosis of active candida overgrowth, according to Dr. Broughton.

Some individuals utilize live cell analysis of the blood for diagnosis. Undoubtedly a larger number of yeast patients are thus uncovered or confirmed. The strong possibility of observer bias, however, and the lack of properly evaluated cases in scientific research limit this technique for reliable, consistent usage. The live cell test may well prove to be a diagnostic test of choice in the future when properly studied by the medical community. The possibility of subjective bias, however, limits its usefulness at the present time.

The patient who responds favorably to treatment (with diet, nystatin, other drugs or more natural therapies) perhaps has the most compelling evidence for the yeast connection.

When a careful history is taken from the patient, when thorough laboratory examination is carried out, when supporting laboratory data are sought and acquired, and when adequate therapy for yeast overgrowth is carried out (including appropriate detoxification, dietary measures and nutrient supplementation) and the results are objectively evaluated, a clinical diagnosis of yeast overgrowth can readily be made or excluded. There is one caveat. No one therapeutic effort must be judged as the single arbiter of success. The patient and the physician must know that all Candida yeasts (like all patients) are not alike in their responsiveness to particular regimens of therapy. Some yeasts, for example, are resistant to nystatin. Therefore, adequate therapy may mean a trial of various treatments. Whenever a yeast organism has been isolated on culture, a differential sensitivity test to various drugs, herbs and other antiyeast chemicals can be supplied by a laboratory that knows the value of such testing. I must point out, too, that patients who improve on "a yeast diet" may do so because they have eliminated significant food allergens or for other reasons. At all times, however, reduction of toxicity and repair of malnutrition are essential maneuvers to bring about favorable change and to support other management measures.

TREATMENT

The most obvious first step in treatment is to remove the cause of the disorder whenever possible. Thus the patient who receives repeated or chronic antibiotic treatments must be brought to a state in which antibiotics are either not required or are used only very rarely. The patient on birth control pills for 10 years must find another form of successful pregnancy prevention or must utilize an aggressive glandular or nutritional program for ovarian support in the case of ovarian insufficiency. The patient with diabetes mellitus must be brought under good control so that high blood sugars are reduced toward normal and sugar in the urine is reduced or eliminated. The patient on therapeutic doses of corticosteroid drugs must be gradually weaned from them, and the disorder being treated must be managed by other appropriate nutritional and glandular means. The patient who consumes an inordinately high carbohydrate diet must be gradually but steadily brought to a lower carbohydrate intake, usually with a concomitant increase in the use of lean animal protein foods. And, of course, as a corollary to carbohydrate lowering, the patient must shift away from simple carbohydrates like sugar and white flour and toward the use of complex carbohydrates such as whole grains and vegetables (see Figure 2).

A book could be written about each of these steps to remove the causes of yeast overgrowth. Suffice it to say here that each of those steps may require long, laborious weeks, months or years to accomplish. And, many times, the cause may not be eradicable because the patient may not desire to undergo the maneuvers necessary to accomplish the task. After all, the yeast connection is a problem of human beings who possess comfortable habits, lifestyles, and attitudes that

Figure 2. The Carbohydrate Hierarchy

WORST FOODS

1. Sweets (simple carbohydrates): Sugars, syrups, honey, corn syrup, maple syrup, high fructose corn syrup, molasses and foods that contain them.

2. Alcoholic beverages

3. Fruit juices

4. Fruits

5. Refined grains ⎫
6. Whole grains ⎭ Breads, Pastas, Cereals Crackers, etc.

7. Legumes and high carbohydrate vegetables (complex carbohydrates)

- •beans
- •peas
- •lentils
- •carrots

- •potatoes
- •sweet potatoes
- •corn on the cob
- •winter squash

- •beets
- •rutabagas
- •turnips
- •artichokes

8. Nonorganic meat, poultry, fish, shellfish

9. Organic meat, poultry, fish, shellfish

10. Low carbohydrate vegetables (organic preferable)

- •romaine
- •parsley
- •cucumbers
- •spinach

- •kale
- •turnip greens
- •beet greens
- •celery

- •asparagus
- •cauliflower
- •broccoli, etc.

BEST FOODS

Higher carbohydrate foods are at the top and to the left. Lower carbohydrate foods are at the bottom and to the right. Meat, poultry, fish and shellfish may be lower in carbohydrates than low carbohydrate vegetables, but they are listed above the latter because of the antibiotics added to their feed. The yeast patient should eat predominantly from levels 8, 9, and 10, but some items from 7 may be eaten in moderation. After successful treatment, the patient may eat from levels 4 and 6. At a still later date, foods from levels 2, 3 and 5 may be used as long as the yeast condition remains dormant. At no time should the patient eat predominantly from levels 1–5.

may not tolerate large degrees of change. Then, too, many yeast patients do not feel well. Thus they may not be able to accomplish large goals quickly. The wise physician must judge the individual patient and the patient's support team to assess the amount and type of therapeutic maneuvers that the patient may be able to invoke. There is nothing worse than demanding too much too soon from a hurting yeast patient, compromised in thought and action and perhaps feeling guilty and inadequate for not following a prescribed therapeutic regimen. Most patients, however, are quite capable of making some dietary improvement and they are usually eager to remove the cause when they understand the disorder and its origins. In actuality, nearly all patients are hungry for guidance in regard to nutritional supplementation and yeast inhibition by nutrients and herbs. Their bodies are so hungry for nutrients because of yeast overgrowth and the interference with the digestion and absorption of food that it so frequently induces.

Some brief comments on each of the suggested treatment areas follow.

DIETARY CHANGE

Dietary change is essential. Sugar-addicted persons must break the habit with help from their nutritional physician. A low carbohydrate diet is always recommended. Even though some patients may get along well on as low as 60 grams of carbohydrate per day, that extreme measure is not necessary. Actually, the patient may improve merely by cutting his bread from four slices a day to two and his pasta from four days to two days a week. Similarly, some patients do well by reducing alcoholic beverages from daily to twice weekly while others may have to renounce all spirits. Fruit juices may be replaced by herbal teas such as taheebo (pau d'arco), huckleberry or ginger tea. Fruits may be reduced from five servings a day to one or two servings a day while the type of fruit is changed from high carbohydrate (bananas, plums, prunes, figs, dates, raisins, grapes) to low carbohydrate (berries, melons or a small apple or grapefruit). See Figure 3 for my suggested diets.

Diet One is the most rigorous in the elimination of carbohydrates. Diet Three is the most liberal. Diet Two occupies a midway position between one and three. Note that these diets do not utilize yogurt or other milk products except in Diet Three where a small portion of skimmed milk on cereal may be used. Some may wish to use these diets as models, but they must always do so with professional supervision. The three diets may also be used as stages in progressive eating, although not all patients must utilize diets One or Two. The diets presented are merely models. There are many other foods that could be utilized. When any such diets are undertaken, the patient must see to it that three meals plus snacks are eaten regularly each day. The length of time that the diet is needed varies with individual patients. The value in such diets is that food allergies and food intolerances can easily be spotted upon reintroductory challenge. Moreover, states of low blood sugar, when they exist, are also effectively managed. Recommended beverages are herbal teas such as taheebo, blueberry, huckleberry, ginger, or pure water with lemon.

The other aspect of diet, of course, is the avoidance of food offenders. When the patient is found to be sensitive to a great many foods, only major allergens must be excluded in order to preserve nutrient sufficiency. Combinations of elimination, reduction in amount and frequency, food desensitizations, and blockade of the allergic response along with intensive nutritional assessment and treatment of gut dysbiosis and "leaky gut" permit the eventual gradual use of a larger variety of foods. Intestinal parasites, when present, must also be eradicated. At all times one must not be blind to the factors other than yeast that determine one's diet. These include psychological, ethnic, nutritional, fiber, cardiovascular, renal, constipative, diarrheal issues and perhaps others. When and if the yeast diet becomes worse than the yeast condition, it's time to reassess the needfulness and severity of the diet. Sometimes patients are the culprits, other times well-meaning physicians or other counselors who demand too much from the patient are to blame. Nutri-

Figure 3

	Diets to Combat Yeast Overgrowth		
	DIET ONE	DIET TWO	DIET THREE
BREAKFAST	Shrimp, almonds, chicken with stir-fry vegetables in olive oil with beans, peas or lentils.	Alternate a whole grain cereal (oatmeal, barley, millet, etc.) with breakfast of Diet One. Use soy, sesame, almond or cashew milk.	Alternate whole grain cereals (oatmeal, barley, millet, rye, etc.) using soy, nut or seed milks with eggs, fish, shrimp and potatoes or yams.
SNACK	1 or 2 eggs.	One serving of low carbohydrate fruit (berries or melon).	One fruit serving of any kind.
LUNCH	Large salad of mixed greens and other vegetables with pumpkin seeds and 1–2 tablespoons of olive oil/lemon juice dressing	As in Diet One with addition of brown rice wafers.	Barley, lentil or miso broth. Large salad with mixed greens and other vegetables, 1–2 Tbsp. of olive oil and sesame seeds.
SNACK	Vegetables, seeds and nuts or nut butter.	As in Diet One.	Vegetables or tofu; seeds, nuts or their butters.
SUPPER	Several noncarbohydrate vegetables, small potato or yam, fish, chicken, turkey or lamb.	As in Diet One.	One or two high carb. vegetables (winter squash, carrots, potatoes, etc.) and one or two low carb vegetables. Turkey, chicken, fish, lamb, beef, eggs.
SNACK	Nuts	As in Diet One.	One fruit of any kind.

tional sufficiency and psychological well-being must be sustained.

I discussed the many issues involved in our cultural addiction to sugar over 15 years ago in my book *Sugar and Your Health*. I recognize the extreme difficulty in wresting sugar away from patients in whom its use is a firmly established cultural habit. Nevertheless, the complete avoidance of sugar in the diet is a major therapeutic tool for treatment of the yeast patient. Patients always ask me, "Need that be forever?" Perhaps not. Only time will tell as periodic ventures into the use of sugar are made in individual cases. My experience suggests that sugar and carbohydrate cravings are eradicated in direct proportion to the control of yeast toxicity and malnutrition.

We in medicine have long known of "candy catarrh," the nose and sinus congestion and drainage that comes from excessive and chronic use of sugar in the diet. Sometimes that congestion stems from allergy to the sugar itself, sometimes from the yeast overgrowth that it provokes and sometimes from the paralytic effect that sugar has on the immune cells charged with ingesting and killing bacteria. After every "dose" of sugar that we consume, the likelihood is that the phagocytic white blood cells will be paralyzed for at least four hours, thus allowing infectious organisms a chance to gain a foothold in the body. The more sugar that we take at one time and the more frequently that we take it, the more likely we are to become overwhelmed in some way by infectious organisms. Remember too that empty-calorie sugar foods displace nutrient-dense foods that support health rather than compromise it.

Now let's look at fat in the diet and its relationship to sugar and carbohydrates. Because we know that excess saturated fats may lead to cardiovascular disease, the diet of every person, including yeast patients, should not contain them. Saturated fats, like sugars, have permeated our culture and they are difficult to avoid. The situation with saturated fats, however, is quite different than that of sugar. For a variety of reasons, the message that cholesterol, total fat and saturated fat are items to be shunned has become common knowledge for nearly all Americans. Therefore, one's task in the reduction/elimination of saturated fats bears the imprimatur of the establishment. The reduction/elimination of sugar, however, is not seen as a particularly serious or health-threatening issue. Despite many warnings, our consumption of empty-calorie sugar remains at 125–135 pounds per year per average person in the United States. Thus we see that this carbohydrate nonfood occupies an enormous niche in the diets of most Americans, whether they realize it or not. That load of sugar has become a major underlying component of the yeast complex. Nevertheless, proper yeast treatment, detoxification and nourishment can support the sugar-craver in turning away from sweets.

In order to prevent the development of fatty acid deficiency from low fat diets (and we are seeing much more of it now than in previous decades), I advocate the use of nonsaturated fats and oils in the daily diet. That follows the recommendations of William C. Willett, M.D., of the Department of Nutrition at Harvard University School of Public Health. When olive oil is used in place of a saturated fat such as the fat in red meats, cheese and butter, the artery-clogging cholesterol (LDL) drops and the artery-clearing cholesterol (HDL) remains the same. What is happening so often in America is that additional carbohydrates (usually refined) are used to replace the saturated fat. In some cases, when individuals fail to obtain sufficient protein, they resort to quick fixes in the form of candies, frozen yogurt or pastries. The additional carbohydrate load often leads to weight gain, low blood sugar and/or grain allergies. In addition, both LDL and HDL are reduced, and that may not be desirable. Moreover, the higher carbohydrate diet gives impetus to yeast overgrowth with all the complications that it can entail.

In order to avoid the overuse of high carbohydrate foods, two food categories must be stressed. Think of lean, animal protein foods and low carbohydrate vegetables (categories 8–10 in Figure 2) as the staples of the diet. Then add to them enough high carbohydrate vegetables, legumes and whole grains (categories 6 and 7) to provide energy needs and satiety. Fruits may also be included, but always in moderation.

Refer again to Figure 3 for three representative meal plans ranging from the most rigorous to the most liberal.

ENVIRONMENTAL CHANGE

Yeast-connection patients usually grow worse in their clinical complaints when their environments are laden with molds. Therefore, careful consideration must be given to identification of the presence of molds and their eradication from the daily environment of such patients. Since food that enters the gastrointestinal tract must be considered part of one's daily environment, fungal foods and foods fermented by molds should be avoided. Eliminating such foods as mushrooms, yeasts, beer, wine, other alcoholic beverages, cheeses, yogurt, pickles, and sometimes peanuts may be beneficial. Also loose cotton underwear that "breathes" must replace pantyhose.

The air in which such patients live can be assessed to determine the "load" of molds that it contains. Special growth-media plates for molds can be exposed in the areas of the home in which yeast-connection patients spend the most time. Usually bedrooms, bathrooms, and perhaps kitchen areas are tested. If very low levels of mold are found, nothing further need be done. If high levels are found, the air-conditioning ducts should be cleaned and treated with mold-killing agents, and the obvious sources of humidity and dampness should be contained. Often, moisture may be found around tubs and sinks. All used towels should be placed immediately into the washer after each use. The walls of the shower and the shower curtain should be dried immediately after each use. Dehumidifiers may help. Humidistats may be needed on air-conditioning systems. Special home treatments for mold may be used. An effective air-filtering system for the home should be installed. HEPA filters and/or electrostatic filters are very helpful, but precise attention must be paid to changing or cleaning the units at recommended intervals. The most effective air-filtering systems, however, shall remain mere helping modes as long as a serious source of mold exposure remains in a home or place of work. It is amazing how much mold growth can occur in wall cracks, around utilities or on and under rugs that have been wet. If there is any doubt about the eradication of mold, then repeat exposure of mold plates for mold cultures will tell the tale. Whenever mold plates do *not* reveal molds but symptoms persist, mold (yeast) *within* the patient (gut, vagina, ears, etc.) may be the cause unless a different source of environmental irritation may be present. Dust, fumes, chemicals, pesticides and animals are all possible culprits.

The Candida mold is not readily airborne, but is easily cultured from toothbrushes, plastic kitchen sponges, tile grout, and plastic shower curtains. It also grows well on formica and on plastic cutting boards. The conclusion is inescapable that natural materials used in the home are less hospitable to Candida than synthetic materials. The same conclusion relates to the human body. When synthetic materials such as refined sugar, birth control pills, antibiotics, refined carbohydrates and corticosteroids are taken in, yeasts have a rich environment in which to grow and multiply. In order to heal, human beings must give up their synthetic surroundings and synthetic inputs and return to the natural balancing principles of earlier days.

Finally, I want to recommend the Living Air Unit, an air-filter unit that also generates a controlled and easily monitored concentration of ozone (see Resources). A variety of models are available that kill mold, neutralize animal danders, kill dust mites, immobilize dust and pollen particles, eliminate smoke and inactivate unwanted pesticides and other household chemicals. Ozone in excessive amounts (more than 200 parts per billion) is of course toxic, and a rare individual is hypersensitive even to small quantities of ozone. The vast majority of persons with yeast overgrowth, however, have allergic reactions to environmental molds. In such cases the markedly decreased quantities of molds and the accompanying decrease, inhibition or eradication of bacteria, dust, pesticides, indoor household chemicals and danders observed with the use of this unit is often dramatic and usually very helpful.

YEAST REMOVAL

The best way to remove yeast from one's body is to deprive it of the carbohydrate food upon which it thrives. Unfortunately, the low levels of carbohydrate intake needed to accomplish that may starve the human host as well as the yeast. Therefore, other measures must be invoked to assist a low carbohydrate intake in dislodging the Candida once and for all.

We can start with the mouth. Commercially available peroxide toothpastes may suppress oral yeast. The exact role of Candida-yeast in the production of periodontal disease has not been delineated. I suspect that it is a strong factor when both the local effects in the mouth and the nutritional and toxic factors from the gut or vagina are considered. Thus the peroxide toothpastes may help at the portal of entry to diminish the burden of yeast overgrowth in the gastrointestinal tract. More certain, I believe, is the practice of Oolitt tongue scraping to mechanically rid the tongue of yeast and other factors (food particles, bacteria, viruses, stagnant secretions) that may foster yeast growth. Scraping the tongue after breakfast and at bedtime every day is a must for the yeast patient and for those who wish to minimize periodontal disease. Besides removing accumulated food debris and germs, the tongue-scraping patient is rewarded by a lower incidence of colds and sore throats. Hence, the need for antibiotics may diminish. An Oolitt plastic scraper may be obtained from Deep Trading Corporation (see Resources). Many substances can be used with the scraping or after the scraping to further discourage yeast growth. Some use goldenseal root powder; I often recommend an effective colloidal silver liquid. Diluted gentian violet may suffice. Often, however, tongue scraping alone suffices. I do not recommend ordinary mouthwashes or undiluted 3 percent hydrogen peroxide except with strict professional supervision. In any case, beware of highly caustic food grade, 35-percent hydrogen peroxide. Attention to the removal of food, plaque and other accumulated debris from the interstices of the teeth via dental flossing, toothpicks, rubber dental picks and other cleansing devices can also help. Be careful, however, lest the zeal to cleanse results in injury to the delicate gums and mucous membranes of the mouth and gums. Be sure also to disinfect mouth tools after use with 3 percent hydrogen peroxide.

In rare cases, the supervising physician may suggest that a total bowel cleansing be performed. Harmless but effective iso-osmotic chemical substances are used for this purpose that, in effect, drain the bowel of all its contents without draining the patient of fluids and electrolytes. Such substances are used to prepare the bowel for intestinal surgery, but I have adapted them as a single quick cleanse to empty the bowel of its yeast. The procedure is not much fun, needless to say, and may need to be repeated for ideal effects. Most patients are more content to utilize a wide variety of bowel cleanses that utilize fiber bulking agents, herbs and friendly bacteria such as acidophilus. Likewise, a series of colonic irrigations may be called for in the initial phase of management. Home enemas and coffee enemas (to produce liver-bile flushing) may also be effective. A number of oral preparations have become available to support liver detoxication and to cleanse the bowel, the usual source of the liver toxicity. Some persons use rectal implants of friendly bacteria. Since both dead and living yeast organisms may play a role in a patient's symptom complex, it is essential to physically remove yeast from the body whenever we may encounter it—on the tongue, under the nails, in the gut and vagina or on the skin. The lower the load of yeast organisms in the body at any one time, the fewer symptoms the patient has and the less likely he or she is to experience yeast die-off under appropriate treatment.

At all times, however, caution must be taken not to cause a new problem while trying to solve an old one. Moderate measures over a longer period are usually much safer than severe measures carried out more quickly. Because of the sometimes subtle hazards of self-care, professional advice is always recommended.

HOMEOPATHIC TREATMENT

The homeopathic approach to yeast overgrowth is often very effective. I use it most often in the initial phases of management to reduce symptoms and to clear the body of toxic potential for reaction if and when therapeutic drugs must be used. A wide variety of preparations is available. Most contain yeast in standard homeopathic dilutions. Homeopathy may also be directed, of course, at acute symptoms, miasms and the constitutional factors inherent within the individual patient. In this way the underlying issues that may have led to the need for recurrent antibiotics can be addressed.

YEAST DESENSITIZATION

An actual allergy to yeast may be a major component of the yeast problem. When that allergy is identified and treated, the patient gets well faster. Therefore, some kind of probe for yeast allergy may be desirable. Allergenic skin tests utilizing Candida-yeast are helpful. Sublingual provocative challenge with measurement of pulse rate and salivary pH can be employed. Blood tests for immunoglobulin E, immunoglobulin G, immunoglobulin G4 and cellular reactions are quite helpful. When environmental and dietary eliminations of yeast are insufficient to alleviate symptoms, then institution of yeast desensitization can be carried out. Injections of diluted yeast antigens, as well as other offending molds, can be carried out by the supervising physician or by an allergist. The use of vaccines that do not contain preservatives is much to be preferred. However, the difficulties attendant upon the production, distribution and maintenance of such vaccines are so great at this time that only a few physicians are able to supply them. Desensitization can also be carried out by the sublingual route. Although standard allergists usually fail to recognize the success of such treatment, the treatment often works with less risk to the patient than injections.

Some persons require long-term Candida-yeast desensitization. I have a number of cases in which desensitization has been carried on for five to ten years. I always advocate the shortest treatment time that is consistent with good results. In patients who require long-term therapy, a relapse may occur when the injections are discontinued. Most persons, however respond well to shorter periods of desensitization, particularly as yeast treatment efforts become more and more effective and environmental control of mold exposures takes hold.

HERBAL YEAST INHIBITION

Many, many herbs can assist in returning the body to good health. Key agents are garlic, goldenseal root, echinacea, gentian, taheebo, ginger, thyme, rosemary, oregano, Oregon grape, barberry, cinnamon, tea tree oil, fennel, citrus seed extract, maitake, tannins and others. The reported side effects of treatment with such herbs are minimal if any. There are many other herbs that enhance the immune system, for example, ganoderma, shitaki, lomatium, St. John's wort and astragalus. They can be used to support the patient's general defenses as more specific measures diminish the yeast load in the body.

Since so much has already been written about the healing properties of echinacea, goldenseal and garlic, I shall direct my remarks to tea tree oil, citrus seed extract and tannins. Tea tree oil (*Malaleuca alternifolia*) is obtained from the leaves of the tea tree, a plant native only to the northeast coastal area of New South Wales, Australia. The oil is an ideal skin anti-infective and may be applied directly to skin, nail fungus or yeast infections. Although skin reactions to it are rare, for "tender" areas of the body I suggest using a few drops of the oil in a teaspoon of olive oil and gradually increasing the strength as tolerated. I have obtained good results in nasal and sinus yeast conditions by having the patient inhale the tea tree oil aroma (not the oil) several times a day. Again, start with a very weak dilution of the tea tree oil in olive oil or water and increase strength as tolerated. See the section on local therapy for the vagina (page 37) for vaginal use.

Citrus seed extract can be obtained in forms suitable for topical use or oral use. Liquids or capsules are available. I have not found a tasty liquid form. Small quantities are not often effective in my experience. For yeast treatment by mouth I suggest at least 125 mg three times a day. Because the anti-infectious spectrum is so broad, good results probably occur because of simultaneous assault upon a large number of other unwanted, "unfriendly" gastrointestinal organisms that cluster along with the yeast overgrowth. If one is also taking "friendly" acidophilus bacteria do so at times other than when citrus seed extract is taken.

Tannins are found in products from the roots and bark of certain plants. Their action is to disrupt the cell wall structure of unwanted organisms and to prevent them from attaching to themselves and to host tissues. Tannin products can be purchased from Intensive Nutrition Products, San Leandro, CA 94577 (see Resources). The capsules for oral antifungal use are called Tanalbit. They are comprised of zinc tannates from Babul bark, Swedish birch bark, Argentinian Quebracho extract, glucosamine derivatives of hydrolyzed chitin extract and Asiatic Holy Lotus rhizome extract. Since viral infections so commonly co-exist with the yeast complex condition (usually as smoldering, low-grade chronic conditions), another tannin product, Viràcin, can also be very helpful in restoring energy to the yeast-overwhelmed individual. The oral and vaginal tannates will be further discussed in the sections on local therapy of the mouth (page 36) and vagina (pages 37–38).

NUTRITIONAL MEASURES AND OTHER THERAPIES

A healthy immune system and a healthy gastrointestinal tract require a full complement of nutrients. In fact, all cells of all tissues in the body require a full complement of nutrients—in optimal supply—in order to function properly year after year without degeneration. In all likelihood, a major element of the aging process is a gradual decrease in the nutriture of the body's tissues and the organs that digest, pump, secrete, circulate and excrete to keep us alive. In that slow but inexorable process of aging decay, unrecognized nutrient deficiencies are likely the biggest single factor that we can correct to retard the aging process. Malnutrition also plays a significant role in yeast overgrowth.

In order to be optimally nourished, one must consume organic (biologically pure) foods in wide varieties. One must also be able to digest and absorb very well. The evidence from my practice is that we are in the midst of an epidemic of functional maldigestion and malabsorption. The reasons are numerous, but again the yeast complex plays a major role. One must also be able to transport the absorbed nutrients in unclogged blood vessels, transmitting them to all cells of the body. With age and an increasingly sedentary lifestyle, large areas of the body tissues may be deprived of these essential blood-borne nutrients. It is as though the arterial highways of a city were progressively shutting down with the result that outlying areas no longer received goods from the central city. One reason may be a lack of demand from relatively metabolically inactive cells such as unused muscles. Faced with poor circulation, the body can malfunction in a variety of ways. Nothing will work as well as it should, and especially vulnerable tissues and organs will be the hardest hit.

What can we do to enhance nutritional delivery to all tissues? We can exercise. We can stretch. We can receive spinal manipulation. We can utilize a variety of other body therapies to release tension; enhance lymph flow; eradicate energy blocks, trigger points and unwanted reflexes; we can learn biofeedback techniques that promote flow within the body.

Among the most valuable body therapies are the systems of reflexology, neuromuscular therapy, myofascial and positional release, craniosacral treatment, acupressure and acupuncture. I view all as different modes of nutritional therapy because they facilitate the transfer of nutrients within the body to a wider expanse of tissues that otherwise would be circulation-deprived and thus nutrient-deprived. The nutrients are, of course, those ingested but also those manufactured within the body—some of which we know and some of which we do not. Perhaps most important of all in facilitating the optimal function of all cells by enhancing their nutrient supply is intravenous E.D.T.A. chelation therapy. Although it is true that this treatment is most often given to older persons with circulatory disorders, I find that an initial course of 10 to 30 chelation treatments given at the onset of yeast therapy improves and even quickens the therapeutic results.

When we consider the nutrients that the yeast patient may require in supplementation, we must first plug the nutritional gaps that we suspect or can prove. For example, a common scenario is to encounter a young woman in her mid- or late-30s, locked into a schedule of long hours at work with little or no time to shop, exercise, prepare meals or rest. Perhaps she is divorced. Perhaps there are childrens' or parents' needs to meet. Commonly, such a patient relies upon coffee, donuts, fast foods, candy bars, cookies or colas for those slump times. It doesn't require the services of a dietitian to guess that vegetables are in very short supply and there are likely to be many other nutrition deficits as well. The point is that one could lecture and admonish all day, yet still the patient would find it difficult to change her fast food, fast-paced lifestyle. Thus it makes sense to promptly supply a bevy of nutritional supplements in addition to any yeast treatments that are undertaken. Although it would be preferable to get these essential nutrients from fresh, organic greens, the first step in such cases is to prescribe capsules or powders that can be quickly and conveniently used. Many patients find that taking customized nutrient supplements is a lifesaver, a start for building a better nutritional lifestyle.

For those persons who wish to scientifically determine the nutrients that they specifically require, a wide variety of nutritional probes is available. It makes sense to utilize such tests whenever possible because we find that no one person has the same nutritional deficits as the next person. Currently I employ the following biochemical probes of nutritional status: complete blood count; automated SMA or multiple blood chemical profile of electrolytes, blood sugar, calcium and phosphorus; liver function tests; blood fats; kidney function tests; hair analysis (pubic); nutrient and toxic minerals in urine, whole blood, serum and red blood cells; intracellular minerals (by scraping the cells of the oral epithelium); vitamins, minerals, and amino acids in live cultured lymphocytes; broad panels of antioxidant measurements; organic acids in urine; and amino acids in blood and urine. Many others are also available.

Assuming that the patient is consuming at least five fresh vegetables and up to two fresh fruits per day and with due appreciation of individual nutrient needs, it is possible to recommend a general program of nutrient supplementation. If the reader holds in mind that variations on these recommendations are commonly needed, the following suggestions may be considered appropriate and safe for the adult, non-pregnant, non-lactating, otherwise healthy female in her menstruating years. All supplements should be free of sugar, starch, dye, yeast, corn, wheat and milk.

Recommended Supplements	
Vitamin A	5,000 I.U.
Beta carotene or mixed carotenoids	5,000 I.U.
Vitamin D3	400 I.U.
Vitamin C	500 mg
Mixed bioflavonoids	100 mg
Vitamin E	400 I.U.
B complex	10–75 mg
Chromium	200 mcg
Iodine	100 mcg
Boron	1 mg
Copper	1–2 mg
Selenium	200 mcg
Molybdenum	100 mcg
Zinc	15-30 mg
Manganese	6 mg
Iron	18 mg
Calcium	500 mg
Magnesium	200 mg

In addition, vegetarians with yeast overgrowth should take an amino acid supplement. A variety of algaes and green food supplements are helpful, or one can use a supplement from other sources such as fish, rice, soy or egg that supply the full range of essential amino acids. All yeast patients should be sure to consume two tablespoons of olive oil daily—added to soups, cereals, vegetables or salads.

There are specific nutrients or nutrient-like materials that inhibit the growth and spread of yeast such as biotin, olive oil, tannins and caprylic acid in time-released form. Undecylenic acid from castor beans can also be used. A bevy of friendly bacteria is needed although these organisms usually need to be accompanied by their necessary growth factors, fructo-oligosaccharides (FOS) and n-acetyl glucosamine. Intestinal antibodies such as those found in the colostrum and milk may also be utilized to enhance immunity in the gut.

LOCAL THERAPIES

In my years as a physician I have come to appreciate the immense impact of local factors upon the various body parts of the human organism. Thus, in the processes of health and disease that determine our status at any point in time, one must diligently attend to local care of body parts as well as general factors. That concept is clearly evident in the treatment of yeast overgrowth. I have many patients who receive systemic drugs to which their yeast is sensitive, yet they persist with local vaginal infections or local gastrointestinal yeast overgrowth. (The converse is also true that successful local treatment in the vagina or gut may fail to eradicate yeast-related symptoms until systemically active pharmacological medications are employed.) As mentioned earlier, a hallmark of successful yeast therapy is intestinal cleansing. Whether by oral colon cleanse, enemas, colonic irrigations, dietary manipulation or combinations of these treatments, the removal of stagnant bowel contents and the insurance of a healthy bowel transit time are key goals for the rest of the patient's life.

I have already referred to Oolitt tongue scraping for local

care in the mouth as well as immaculate tooth and gum care. Courses of other therapies may be needed for oral thrush or esophageal candidiasis. Any of the antiyeast herbs may be used in powder or liquid forms, although most are not palatable and the resultant, temporary discoloration of the mouth may be cosmetically unacceptable. Colloidal silver comes in a liquid form and has an acceptable taste. The prescription drug, nystatin, has long been used. Nystatin powder mixed in water can be held in the mouth, swished thoroughly, and swallowed after meals and at bedtime. Because of its bitter taste, nystatin may not be suitable for infants and children. As far as I'm aware, there exists no commercial preparation of nystatin for small children that does not contain sugar as a sweetener along with various dyes and other chemical compounds. Although such preparations are distinctly undesirable, their use can be so effective that they need to be utilized despite their drawbacks. Lozenges of clotrimazole are theoretically effective, but their track record has not been great in my experience. A one-percent solution of gentian violet, diluted with an equal quantity of water, can be used to paint the mouth, resulting in an intense violet color which stains the mouth. Professional guidance is strongly recommended for all of these procedures.

Herbal preparations available for oral use can be quite effective (see Resources). The preparation Tanoral is a mint-flavored powder that can be mixed with water for mouth rinsing, gargling or toothbrushing. Orithrush, a dilute solution of potassium sorbate, can be used undiluted as a mouthwash and gargle after meals and at bedtime. Neither preparation should be swallowed.

The local treatment of the gut between the mouth and the anus is the province of diet, detoxification, bowel cleansing, "friendly" bacteria, herbals, other yeast inhibiters and medications. These have been addressed in other sections. Here, however, I wish to stress the efficacy of the caprylic acid preparations. Usually, when the dose is adequate, caprylic acid will effectively suppress yeast overgrowth. I prefer timed-release preparations at a dose of 680 mg per tablet, two tablets three times a day. Mild cases or small individuals may be able to use lesser strengths or amounts. The anus and rectum must also sometimes be treated. The same type of preparations may be employed. Nystatin topical cream (a prescription item) is convenient and can be carried in a purse or pocket. Tea tree oil, suitably diluted if need be, can be applied to the peri-anal area. Anal itching may be caused by pinworms, bacterial infections, other fungi, other parasites, bowel pH disturbances or food allergies, but the source is more likely to be candida-yeast. Nystatin retention enemas using pure nystatin powder in water may also be employed.

Local treatment of the vagina is commonly needed in order to adequately eliminate the direct and indirect effects of the yeast syndrome. Gynecologists often see women who return month after month for refills on their prescriptions for local vaginal care. More local, antiyeast medications are now available over the counter. Gynecologists as a whole (with significant exceptions) fail to recognize the yeast connection in its entirety. More and more, however, they are coming to realize that courses of oral nystatin, short courses of oral ketoconazol (Nizoral), and single-dose, oral fluconazole (Diflucan) are most helpful to women who fail to solve their vaginal yeast infections with the intravaginal prescription medications available. We must recognize at this point that all that discharges, itches and hurts is not caused by yeast. Nevertheless, in our day and age, most are. Proper gynecological diagnosis is certainly desirable. I must point out, however, that the absence of yeast on smears of vaginal secretions and in vaginal cultures does *not* exclude yeast as a culprit. Whenever possible, the male sexual partner should be simultaneously treated.

A variety of natural therapies may interdict yeast overgrowth in the warm, wet, dark vaginal spaces. At the same time, the woman's diet should be free of sugar and refined carbohydrates. Plain yogurt mixed with enough water to permit its introduction into the vagina via douching may be very effective. Powders of lactobacillus acidophilus may be mixed with water for the same purpose. Taheebo or goldenseal root capsules may be mixed with water for vaginal douching. Colloidal silver may likewise be irrigated into the vagina once or twice daily.

Crushed or minced fresh garlic may be suspended for an hour in just-boiled water, strained, and used. When orithrush D (for douche), a liquid concentrate of the potassium salt of sorbic acid, is diluted in water an excellent antifungal douche is obtained (see Resources). Tea tree oil can also be used in a vaginal douche. I suggest starting with only a few drops of the oil in 1 cup of water. If there are no adverse reactions, then the concentration can gradually be increased as tolerated up to a tablespoon of oil in a cup of water if the vaginal problem requires it. However, in my experience, that strength is rarely required. Some women respond nicely to 1 or 2 drops of tea tree oil on a tampon. At all times with any of the vaginal douches, treatment should only be temporary. If long term treatment is required, the safest is the use of plain yogurt with live acidophilus culture or suitable powder or liquid acidophilus preparations.

Nystatin, in my experience, has been very effective. The problem is how to get the powder to stay in the vagina, since the best results occur when nystatin powder stays in contact with the vaginal walls on a constant basis over three to six weeks. For women who do not mind wearing tampons, nystatin powder on a tampon can be used. A sticky lubricant is applied to the tampon. The nystatin powder is liberally applied to it, and the tampon is worn continuously (changed every six to eight hours) for three to six weeks at the same time that oral nystatin or other yeast treatment measures are utilized. The use of nystatin topical cream or powder to the vulva and the entire perineum enhances the therapeutic effect. When the male partner can be enjoined to use the topical nystatin cream on the penis during sexual relations, additional benefit occurs. Immaculate perineal hygiene and drying helps, of course, but is often overlooked as a significant feature in treatment. Douching with liquid garlic preparations may also be used. Some advocate inserting a clove of raw garlic in the vagina daily.

One of the excellent benefits of adequately treating yeast overgrowth is the reduction or elimination of repeated urinary tract infections in the female. The local measures already indicated may be all that is needed. At other times, however, systemic drugs such as ketoconazole, fluconazole or itraconazole are needed. Often helpful is the application of a few drops of a potent colloidal silver preparation to the urinary opening within the vulva morning and evening.

Many other local areas of the body can be treated by anti-yeast measures. On the skin, nails and in the ears, 3-percent hydrogen peroxide works well. Liquid garlic in the ear canals, perhaps used in conjunction with DMSO, as well as nystatin powder and DMSO can be excellent. The prescription solution of clotrimazole (Lotrimin) has given excellent results in ears and on skin yeast rashes. Resistant nail fungus infections may respond to fluconazole in DMSO painted on the nails several times daily. Orithrush D can be used undiluted on skin, nails and in ears with good success.

BOWEL REHABILITATION

The combined effects of yeast overgrowth, food allergies, toxins, parasites, intestinal dysbiosis and subnourishment nearly always invoke faulty function of the gut that threatens to remain with the patient indefinitely after the yeast is contained. Hence a strong effort must be directed at improving the function of the gut, the lifeline for each and every one of us. Learning to make a lifelong habit of eating responsibly is the key to success. That does not necessarily mean that patients with yeast overgrowth must maintain dietary rigidity the rest of their lives. It does mean that once successfully treated, they must learn how to stay below their individual threshold for yeast relapse. Many yeast patients can tell immediately, by the return of their old symptoms, when that threshold has been crossed. Others, however, must rely upon diagnostic probes such as yeast immune complexes, yeast antibodies, or stool and vaginal cultures performed by a laboratory that diligently searches for and quantifies the amount of yeast present.

The supplement industry has provided us with the nutrient items and combinations that promote the restoration of damaged gut cells to normal. These items include n-acetyl-gluscosamine, n-acetyl cysteine, glutathione, butyrates, fructo-oligosaccharides, the wide variety of "friendly bacteria," glutamine, biotin, gamma-linolenic acid, gamma oryzanol and phosphatidyl choline. Undoubtedly others shall be forthcoming. A wide variety of soluble and insoluble fibers are also desirable in the diet or as supplements. One can measure the presence of leaky gut, intestinal maldigestion and malabsorption and intestinal dysbiosis by repeated comprehensive digestive stool analysis, intensive parasite exams and mucosal permeability testings. Naturally, all intestinal parasites must be eliminated. Contamination of the upper bowel by unwanted bacterial growth may be tested for by breath analysis and subsequently treated when present. At all times a strong presence of a variety of friendly bacteria, must be maintained in the gut. Replacement hydrochloric acid as well as vitamins B_{12} and folic acid may be crucial factors in restoring normal gut ecology and mucous membrane function. The importance of a healthy intestinal transit time (eight to twelve hours) and avoidance of constipation must be emphasized. Juice Plus (see Resources) combine in one preparation the enzymes, fibers and flora that usually clear bowel problems and nourish the body at the same time.

MEDICATIONS

Whenever possible, natural therapies such as diet, herbs, nutrient supplements and friendly bacteria along with discontinuance of yeast-promoting activities are recommended. A disturbing attitude, however, has arisen in some quarters. Some advocates of natural therapies have begun to denigrate the use of prescription drugs—including the least toxic drug of all—nystatin. Although such zealous advocates of the "natural" approach undoubtedly are well-meaning, withholding nystatin would deal a serious blow to the cause of beleaguered yeast patients. Every physician wishes to select treatment with the most favorable risk/benefit ratio for his patient. In the case of nystatin, the physician possesses a remarkably safe and effective drug. Then, too, the physician must consider the risk of *not* using the drug as well as the risk of using it. When used selectively for the patient who is not open to natural therapies, nystatin, in about 80 to 85 percent of cases, is most effective and almost never toxic. The fact that nystatin is essentially not absorbed from the gut may account for its remarkable track record of safety. It is, of course, a natural product itself, and that may also be why it possesses so little toxicity. As with any natural substance, however, some persons are allergic to nystatin.

A natural "medication" to try is colloidal silver. In the colloidal form, silver is considered a medication, although it is so safe that it does not require a prescription. However, long term use may result in a bluish coloring of the skin. Silver has an excellent topical action, hence its use in treating burn victims. I prefer a 40 part per million strength colloidal silver preparation for use orally and topically for yeast treatment. Treatment should be continued for up to three months. Consult a competent professional for dosage.

Ketoconazole (Nizoral), fluconazole (Diflucan), itraconazole (Sporanox) and the wide variety of prescription vaginal preparations are invaluable for some patients. These drugs must be used cautiously, and a high index of suspicion for liver damage must always be entertained. I, for one, insist upon a set of blood chemistries before embarking upon such drug treatments and every few weeks thereafter for the duration of the treatments. In addition, the prescribing physician and patient must know that ketoconazole, fluconazole and itraconazole are notorious for interfering with the metabolism of other drugs. They inhibit metabolic liver enzymes and thus may allow levels of certain other drugs to build to toxic levels. Properly used and monitored, however, these drugs can be strongly recommended when other measures fail or when the patient will not or cannot utilize potentially safer therapies.

Jonathan's Story
Jonathan's mother was an astute registered nurse. At four years of age, her son was plagued with recurrent allergies that manifested as chronic runny nose, intermittent rashes,

irritability and itching. Many types of antiallergic treatments had been used. Jonathan also had frequent bacterial infections of the nose, throat, ears and bronchial tubes that required repeated courses of antibiotics. At times, the use of antibiotics was sustained over several months in order to keep him clear of infections. As a result of allergy tests by several doctors, Jonathan was found to be allergic to a large number of foods and some pollens, molds and dusts. Attempts to withdraw the food offenders and to desensitize the boy with allergic desensitizing injections had not been helpful. Many elaborate filtering devices had been installed in the boy's home and bedroom to provide clean air free from dust and molds. The ducts of the air conditioning and heating systems had been thoroughly cleaned on a yearly basis. Still Jonathan had major allergic symptoms and required antibiotics at least six times per year.

When I saw the boy at four years of age he appeared poorly nourished. His hair lacked luster. Dark circles were prominent under his eyes. His growth rate was borderline. Body fat was sparse. His eyes were dull. His skin was dry and flaky. Jonathan's mother stated that whenever he received an antibiotic, he became hyperactive. Moreover, in recent months the hyperactivity failed to disappear when the antibiotics were stopped.

Primarily because of Jonathan's clinical history, I suggested a therapeutic trial of nystatin. Nutritional supplements free of dyes, colors, flavors, sugar and yeast were also given. Within a month Jonathan was free of all symptoms. The chronic runny nose disappeared; Jonathan was no longer hyperactive, there were no rashes, he was not irritable and he did not itch. In addition, his mother noted that his thought process and general development seemed to take a spurt. Most important was the newly developed tolerance that the child displayed to foods that previously had invoked various allergic symptoms. In other words, his mother was able to provide him with a much wider choice of nutritional foods. His appetite also improved.

After three months of nystatin treatment, the nystatin was discontinued. Within the next two to three months the familiar symptoms of runny nose, hyperactivity, intermittent rashes, irritability and itching returned. As the season changed from summer to fall and into winter, the lad required several antibiotics for persistent nose and throat infections. After a bad winter with illnesses as described, the boy was seen again by me, and the nystatin treatment was again prescribed, primarily because of the history of repetitive use of antibiotics and the suspicion that yeast overgrowth played an etiological role in the boy's condition. Again, Jonathan responded promptly and lost all symptoms. This time the nystatin was continued for a six-month period, at first in a full treatment dose and later in a small preventive dose. He has required no further antibiotics and remains symptom-free.

Barbara's Story

Having had the problem of chronic/recurrent vaginal yeast infections over at least 15 years Barbara at 45, sought help because her memory was fading, her sexual relations with her husband were painful and her urination was frequent, urgent and stinging. She had used a wide variety of yeast therapies in the past to little or no avail. She had been treated with a large number of intravaginal creams with minimal results.

I conducted tests of blood sugar, blood and urine and found no blood sugar abnormalities, no anemia, no liver dysfunction and no bacterial urinary infection. Thyroid function was low, and blood indicators of menopause were present. Barbara was treated with fluconazole (Diflucan) 200 mg/tablet, one tablet taken once a week for four weeks. After the first tablet, her urinary symptoms disappeared and, for the first time in years, sex was enjoyable. As her blood liver function tests were followed and found to be normal, another six weeks of drug therapy was given. By the end of that period, her memory had improved by more than 75 percent. Moreover, a new availability of energy now permitted her to improve her diet and replace refined carbohydrates with more nutritious choices. She also was able to organize her energy and thinking for task completion with the result that her moldy house could be appropriately cleaned and altered to reduce environmental mold.

Barbara needed a quick stroke for relief. She needed the services of a prescription drug that could enter the entire body to act quickly on bladder, vagina and presumably, brain. By utilization of the drug in small but significant amounts, the keys were turned to unlock other helping areas.

Medical treatment with prescription drugs more often brings on the so-called yeast die-off condition than more natural treatments do. When yeast die-off occurs, the patient does not feel well at all. Commonly, when drug treatment is commenced slowly and gradually, yeast die-off can be eliminated or greatly minimized. Incidentally, the presence of die-off symptoms supplies the supervising physician with indirect evidence that he is, indeed, dealing with yeast overgrowth.

Connie's Story
Medication is not always needed, as Connie's story illustrates. Connie, a teenager, suffered with terrible PMS, accompanied with bloating, indigestion and headache. Also, her ears and vagina itched in the week before her menstrual periods were due. Because she was anxious to feel better, she willingly improved her diet, took a few nutritional supplements and took a timed-release caprylic acid preparation with every meal. Prompt improvement occurred. Within three months her symptoms had diminished by at least 85 percent. She received no medications. I have seen many, many "Connies" who were able to resolve their yeast overgrowth symptoms with the many natural approaches that have been noted in this booklet. Sometimes, however, home therapies merely remove the tip of the iceberg. In such cases, the next life crisis, emotional setback, viral infection, trauma, move or loss may awaken the indolent, sleeping beast within that we know as the yeast complex.

Case studies can teach us a lot. I deeply believe that this method of clinical research is every bit as important as the strictly scientific, double-blind, crossover study of academic research. Need we do away with the former? No. Need we incorporate the latter? Yes.

John's Story

John was 23 when he complained of pain in the testicles, groin and lower abdomen as well as headaches, blood in the stool, numbness in his body, disturbed sleep, sinus pressure and fatigue that interfered with work. He was unable to work at all. His history revealed that he had taken tetracycline antibiotic for four years from age 18 to 22 for treatment of acne. He had also been given a wide variety of antibiotics because of associated hernia surgery. Large amounts of budding yeasts had been seen in his urine. He improved more and more as he was treated first with nystatin, then ketoconazole and finally fluconazole. He gradually learned the importance of dietary factors in controlling his symptoms. When last seen shortly before this writing, he was improved by 50 to 70 percent and was able to work 30 hours per week. He consumed no sugar, juices, bread or alcohol and ate minimal amounts of cereals and fruits. He knew the value of fluconazole (Diflucan). On several occasions he had been unable to continue its use. At those times all of the old yeast-complex symptoms returned. He probably will require another three to six months of drug therapy and an antiyeast diet to become as well as we want. Whether he will ever be fully rid of the yeast, however, is problematical. We will attempt to rehabilitate the bowel after the intensive yeast drug therapy has concluded. With our rapidly progressing ability to favorably influence nourishment, it is likely that John will eventually become completely drug free and hopefully attain normal bowel function.

MANAGEMENT OF ASSOCIATED CONDITIONS

I have already emphasized that yeast overgrowth is only one component of a multifaceted disease process. A broad-based consideration of the need for simultaneous management of any associated conditions must be made, but priorities must be recognized because patients may be able to tolerate only a small amount of change at any one time. Remember, the yeast complex is a disease process that renders patients vulnerable to stress and excessive demands.

Some yeast patients are depressed and need antidepressants. Others can manage by using antidepressant amino acids and other nutrients. Any adrenal and gonadal insufficiencies must be addressed. When thyroid replacement is needed, very little else is accomplished until that occurs. Autoimmune thyroiditis is present with inordinate frequency in yeast patients. Food allergies, mercury fillings and chemical sensitivities may prove to be major elements that, when properly addressed, will permit large leaps of progress in yeast control. Often the Epstein-Barr virus or some other viral infection must be eliminated. Viràcin can be most helpful in combination with appropriate yeast treatment. (see Resources). Nutritional adequacies and body, liver and bowel detoxifications are essential for therapeutic success. Often, but not always, bowel and body toxin reductions are the first order of business in treatment.

Towering over all these factors, however, is the mammoth one of optimal nourishment. That is such a difficult goal to achieve in our convenience-oriented, rapid-paced society, that most of the time optimal nourishment is cast aside like an old boot at the side of the road. I am hopeful that this booklet will provide the tools and perspectives needed to conquer the complexities of candida-yeast. By their use we can don a new pair of boots to stride healthfully and comfortably along the path of wellness with friends, family and loved ones.

APPENDIX

RECOMMENDED READING

Crook, William G. *Chronic Fatigue Syndrome and the Yeast Connection*. Jackson, TN: Professional Books, Inc., 1992.

Crook, William G. *The Yeast Connection Handbook*. Jackson, TN: Professional Books, Inc., 1997.

Truss, C. Orian. *The Missing Diagnosis*. Self-published. 1983. Available from the author at P.O. Box 26508, Birmingham, AL 35226.

Willett, W.C. "Mediterrannean Diet Pyramid: A Cultural Model For Healthy Eating." *American Journal of Clinical Nutrition*, 1995; 61 (Supplement): 1402S-6S. #22553.

Wunderlich, Ray C. Jr. *Natural Alternatives to Antibiotics*. New Canaan, CT: Keats Publishing, Inc., 1995.

Wunderlich, Ray C. Jr. *Sugar and Your Health*. St. Petersburg, FL: Good Health Publications, Johnny Reads, Inc., 1982.

RESOURCES

Antibody Assay Laboratories
1715 Wilshire Boulevard
Santa Ana, CA 92705

Great Smokies Diagnostic Laboratory
184 Regent Park
Asheville, NC 28806

Meridian Valley Clinical Laboratory
24030 132nd Avenue S.E.
Kent, WA 98042

Deep Trading Corporation
P.O. Box 273653
Tampa, FL 33688
Tel.: 813–931–0390

Living Air Units:
Alpine Industries
9199 Central Avenue N.E.
Blaine, MN 55434–3422

Juice Plus:
National Safety Associates
Memphis, TN 38118
1–800–347–5947

Tanoral or Viracin
Intensive Nutrition Products
San Leandro, CA 94577
1–800–333–7414

Orithrush:
Cardiovascular Research, Ltd.
1061–B Shary Circle
Concord, CA 94518